Small Cries

Samantha Jackson
Small Cries

20/20 **EYEWEAR**
PAMPHLET SERIES
2015

First published in 2015 by Eyewear Publishing Ltd
74 Leith Mansions, Grantully Road
London W9 1LJ United Kingdom

Typeset with graphic design by Edwin Smet
Printed in England by Lightning Source
All rights reserved © 2015 *Samantha Jackson*
The right of Samantha Jackson to be identified as author of this work has been asserted
in accordance with section 77 of the Copyright, Designs and Patents Act 1988

ISBN 978-1-908998-65-1
WWW.EYEWEARPUBLISHING.COM

With thanks for support and advice to Patience Agbabi and the Arvon/Jerwood mentee group of 2013-2014; Eva Salzman and Francis Spufford at Goldsmiths; Todd Swift and the Maida Vale Poets; Tamar Yoseloff and the Wednesday group. Finally, thanks to Katy Carr and my partner Simon.

for Grace

Your children are not your children.
They are the sons and daughters of Life's longing for itself.
They come through you but not from you,
And though they are with you yet they belong not to you.

from *The Prophet*, Kahlil Gibran

Table of contents

9   *Daddy-long-legs*
10 *Flight Path*
11 *Running*
12 *Kiss*
13 *Milestones*
14 *Blossom*
15 *Teething*
16 *The Fall*
17 *Swimming Lessons*
18 *Conkers*
19 *Pink grapefruits*
20 *Butter-coloured-flies*
21 *Da*
22 *Lullaby*
23 *Slinky*
24 *First Shoes*
25 *Ruskin Park*
26 *On Brighton Beach*
27 *We look in the mirror*
28 *In the taxi to the hospital*

31 *Acknowledgements*

Daddy-long-legs

Every day for a week, at the end of the summer,
they drift in, drawn off course by spotlights
in our kitchen, settle on sideboards, walls,
even the middle of the floor.

Wings too short, legs too long, there's something
about the way they lurch into flight, falter against
the currents of still air. Years ago I would have
squashed them, crushed their frail limbs

beneath my slipper, thread legs splayed across
my bedroom wall – a neat swipe of tissue
and only a powdery smudge of what had been.
Tonight, wings brush softly inside a lampshade,

legs tap up and down the wall, tracing the limits
of their brief existence. I collect them, one by one,
their quiet struggle flickering inside my palms,
offer them up to the warm September night.

Flight Path

As she sleeps in her cot, I listen to the planes
turn, their engines shifting to a lower gear;
a persistent thunder as one tails the other
in a loud cycle of slow ploughed air. If she
was awake she'd claim them, practise the scale
of her voice against the pale morning's din.

Running

How exotic those Sunday morning runs
seem now I'm ushered into consciousness,
into a cascade of duties by her small cries.

Always best in winter, the cool air playing
on my cheeks, before anyone else had woken,
the whole world asleep. My breath steaming in front,

a comforting sign of contact as if nature
answered back, and my legs effortlessly carrying me,
a buoyed passenger given to whichever

direction they might take. I always sensed the river
like a sea, before I saw it; air a little thinner,
looser perhaps, a touch of wind

lifting at the edges. Not salt tang, more sediment,
stir of mineral, scent of industry: for the first time
I was in the city. On the suspension bridge

a photographer might wait to catch the nuance
of new light, on the shred of beach below
a stray couple from a night club might clutch

each other, wrecked beneath a sky almost too blue,
too full of hope. And why would I turn back,
just then, the path glittering as it was in the January sun?

Kiss

Perhaps because you were still woozy
from broken sleep, half dreaming,

half forgetting her morning milk,
you wandered in, nightshirt back to

front, pressed your lips up to the glass,
where I, naked, under the warm fall

of water, met you, from the other side.
Sealed in imagined touch, eyes closed,

mouths soft, yielding to this plate
of cool, it was like nothing stood

between us. Outside, meanwhile,
was turning light and with it, as sure

as the early song of birds, her calling
us back; *mummy, daddy*.

Milestones

Just as you learn your body is a weight
you can lever over, his brain begins
its descent, closing one door after another.
Just as you discover the tool of a hand,
how small fingers can pincer
a whole honey-suckle head, he yanks
the plastic tube from his nose and won't
accept dinner without a plate. Just as
you feel the wobble of your height
stacked on two tiny feet, he waves
his arms around his head, his body
lost to the sea. And I remember
we would race to the end of the garden,
to the bamboo grove of sweet peas
and broad beans, and he would sit me
on his knee, place the pod inside my hand,
watch as I cracked the crisp green open,
found new beans nestled
in the skin, saw how as one life passes
another is ready to begin.

Blossom

has settled in drifts along the road, heaps
into banks of soil, drains, streams across
pavements, car roofs; a light wind stirs
and new petals release, ease into the air,
eager to take flight, give themselves up:
the blank grey sky, for a moment, is held
in celebration, a confetti-effect of pink
and white, where anything seems possible.

Teething

Saliva strings, loosens, pools over
can no longer be held by the tongue.
Cheeks and chin are flush with a steady fire
rising from the gums. Buds,
yet to cut, wait in swollen pockets;
the tooth's face a muted white ghosting out
behind pink. No one knows, for certain,
when they'll come, lever up from the roots,
surface in the mouth wet air.
When a web of ligaments will lace
and contract, start a dance in motion,
shimmy the tooth to the jaw floor.
So we wait, like a birth, for the first
bone-glint, for darkness to
break in the ascent towards light.

The Fall

A split second slows to a series of frames,
I'm somewhere behind a lens, distanced

by glass, as she curls her toes, lowers
her knees, propels from her feet:

arms wide open as she dives her hands
past the mound of pillows I'd placed

to keep her safe, over the edge
of the mattress to the ground she believes

is near, her torso turning now, mid-flight,
the weight of her head angling down towards

the parquet floor, its high polish glittering
a dark promise of what is to come

as my palms wrap around her, too late
to save her jaw from hitting

and I lift her, blood spilling
from behind her two milk teeth

see how it runs, over her, all over me.

Swimming Lessons

As the other children sing and splash,
run laughing in and out of the water,
she clings to your shoulders like a life raft,
teeth chattering, blue lips shouting *No*.

The next time you think you've cracked it,
and even she's convinced, chest puffed,
parading the little wet suit like a party dress
around her room. But when you get there

it's as if her fear was sealed in further,
she won't even put a toe in the water,
her face pressed against your neck.
And you, happiest diving headlong

into surging waves, salt bite of the Atlantic
sparkling in your throat, on your skin,
can't understand it, why she's more like me
than you.

Conkers

Packed in the neck of a vase, they form
a dark cobbled huddle reaching up
to where the glass gives way, flutes out.

Not ornamental, like an arrangement
of pebbles you might find in a waiting room,
a serene layering of pale stone on stone,

they are in a jam, captured with no place
to root, tawny eyes looking this way
and that. More accidental experiment

than still life — small hands that couldn't
resist the woody *plop* — a thick fur already
climbing from the bottom, sped along by

sun on the sill. Even those at the top,
held only yesterday, bear the tell-tale signs
of spores taking full advantage;

a fine white near invisible covering
settled on the next ones to go.

Pink grapefruits

halved, sugared, segments loosened
with a knife, an assortment of cereal packets
and my grandfather, tea towel slung
over one shoulder, wafting in and out
taking our orders. A silver plate of bacon
and tomatoes in a swirl of oiled water,
toast resting in a rack. What brings him
finally to sitting are the scones he releases,
still warm, in the middle of the table.
Ooze of jam-slurred butter on our fingers,
as we sit in silence, swilling each bite back
with milky tea. Here now, I sit at the head
of the table, too many empty seats,
a plate of scones not quite risen. I bite into
the bittersweet of currants caught in the cooking,
a double taste of comfort and discomfort,
and my daughter, persistent as a drum,
asking for more.

Butter-coloured-flies

You sit on the grass slope, she's tucked
in the fold of your lap, her eyes wide as you
whisper *listen* and *wait*. A distant drill from the woods
and you say *woodpecker*, and she, joining one sound to
another, mouths the new word, testing its shape.

When the butterflies come, stirred from sleep
by the warmth in the glade, they weave the air,
wings like sun, butter-coloured-flies,
and she remembers, catches this word,
releases it, carefully.

Da

He's come, he says, to forge the bond,
bath bubbles, toy helicopter at the ready.

But there's no need: Da she shouts
pointing past me to him, her tongue

not muscled enough to curl the 'r'
in Grandad. Perhaps it's the accent,

the Scouse 'ew' he shares with her father.
Maybe it's the way he picks her up,

the confident scoop of a long-time parent.
Or maybe she's sensed something,

a parallel perhaps, she being at the start,
he being at the end, both with an eye

on the changing horizon.

Lullaby

She sends herself to sleep with her voice,
a single note hummed through blanket
and thumb, holding its thread into the dark.

Her fear of sleep came early, not stalled by
teddies, baby dolls, elephants hung from
a mobile, soft lulling shapes swirling above.

Once I heard sobbing, crept in to find her
curled in the corner of the cot, her whole body
taken in a sad sway of sound. They say

sleep is a kind of dying and these days
the word is never mentioned without measure,
baby sleep, little sleep, and a promise

to wake her, that I can't always keep.

Slinky

Here is inertia; a column of steel coils
stationed, going nowhere, drawn
by a residing force to stay as it is.

Hard to see where one coil starts
and another begins; they are
the making and unmaking of each other.

And here is potential: a hub of energy
stored like a bullet; so much to happen
so much not yet happened.

Given the chance, it can propagate waves,
ripple forwards in a flip-flop motion
of top lifting bottom, bottom

lifting top. Not just a mathematical display
of gravity changing energy into
momentum, there's a magic about this

small spring quietly walking.

First Shoes

She sways, staggers, arches her back,
near-to-topple, using the base of her spine
to steady her step. Her feet, still so small,
now loaded, are drawn to the floor.
Gravity is against her, its invisible glue
unbalances what was wobbly before
into a series of challenging lifts.
In this landscape of shoe,
the ground distanced beneath her,
numbed by a layer of rubber and sponge,
each step is a risk as she rolls from
her heels to her toes, presses into
what she doesn't yet know.
It's learning to walk all over again
with a twist, and we watch
as she learns to manoeuvre
this inexplicable weight,
trust in the physics,
in the answer not the problem.

Ruskin Park

I carry her on my shoulders, her hands hooked
beneath my chin as she talks, not to me, not to anyone,
her mind roaming over this seashell, that teddy bear,
the biscuits and spaghetti she might have for her dinner,
stars, owls, boats, fragments of song. We walk through
drifts of pale leaves, across split seedpods squashed on tarmac,
new conkers gleaming inside. Her voice ripples into
the evening air and the sky, just as the sun has sunk,
is luminous, streaked with a brilliant pink.

On Brighton Beach

you search for skimmers, smoothed ovals
the shape of sea-wear. Kneading each stone
in your palm, fingers curled on the curves,
you feel for possibility. When you reach
the water's edge, body sloped, wrist tilted,
concentration laps over you and you spin
the stone towards the horizon. Meanwhile
she drops handfuls of pebbles in a pool
left by the tide, afraid to look at the sea,
unaware of you willing this one stone on,
willing it to go further, to defy the pull
of water, the resistance of air.

We look in the mirror

and smile together, her puffed cheeks
red with play, knotty blond hair scented
with the wind and cold of outside.
Blue eyes, darker than mine, take in
the reflection, mesmerised by her own face.
When she was a baby, she watched herself
cry in the bath, scrunched features
caught and distorted in the silver tap.
She cried, it seemed, to see what crying
looked like, learning controls of cause
and effect. Her hand brushes a twist
of fallen hair from her forehead, and perhaps
the first flicker of self-consciousness,
not yet, I hope, not yet.

In the taxi to the hospital

as my mother presses a plastic bag to
her mouth, curls towards the open window

I should be holding her hand, saying,
like someone else might say, *it's going to be okay*

we'll be there soon. I stare straight ahead,
the driver darting looks in the mirror,

his perfect leather seats, the long space between us—
my useless fingers clenching keys, lip salve,

anything in my pockets. Sometimes I kiss
my own daughter too much, squash her cheek

into my cheek, cup her foot inside my hands.
Later, as the antibiotics start to kick in, a new wave

of nausea sends her sideways; I catch her,
take my mother for the first time in my arms.

Last Call — The Life

The phone — it's unexpected.
He never phones.

How are you I say.

It's a stilted conversation.

His silence grown to a deep sad
                    indifference.
                              A Berlin Wall
Between us an unbridgeable
    Gyrsfo like gaps. Was it what
                              we lack?
We're two people now who lost
    something the real piece of
       family
    the thread, the power to
      future son   connect.

The operation on Friday 12th December
                     I hear
but then occurred   him say. Back for Christmas maybe
do or itt drop then he drops his guard. looks after him
              How does he feel?
However I can tell he's nervous
        but he says he OK — at least he'll
                                be back for Xmas
That was it. He's Nowords ever
                         again.
    He never did make Christmas Day.

Acknowledgements

Thanks to the editors of the following in which versions of the poems originally appeared: *ARTEMISpoetry*, *Swimming Lessons (Jerwood/Arvon Mentoring Scheme: Anthology Volume Four)* and *The Rialto*.

Thanks also to the poem 'Mayflies' by Jeffrey Harrison which advised my poem 'Daddy-long-legs'.

EYEWEAR PUBLISHING

EYEWEAR PAMPHLET SERIES

- **BEN STAINTON** EDIBLES
- **MEL PRYOR** DRAWN ON WATER
- **MICHAEL BROWN** UNDERSONG
- **MATT HOWARD** THE ORGAN BOX
- **RACHAEL M NICHOLAS** SOMEWHERE NEAR IN THE DARK
- **BETH TICHBORNE** HUNGRY FOR AIR
- **GALE BURNS** OPAL EYE
- **PIOTR FLORCZYK** BAREFOOT
- **LEILANIE STEWART** A MODEL ARCHAEOLOGIST
- **SHELLEY ROCHE-JACQUES** RIPENING DARK
- **SAMANTHA JACKSON** SMALL CRIES

EYEWEAR POETRY

- **MORGAN HARLOW** MIDWEST RITUAL BURNING
- **KATE NOAKES** CAPE TOWN
- **RICHARD LAMBERT** NIGHT JOURNEY
- **SIMON JARVIS** EIGHTEEN POEMS
- **ELSPETH SMITH** DANGEROUS CAKES
- **CALEB KLACES** BOTTLED AIR
- **GEORGE ELLIOTT CLARKE** ILLICIT SONNETS
- **HANS VAN DE WAARSENBURG** THE PAST IS NEVER DEAD
- **DAVID SHOOK** OUR OBSIDIAN TONGUES
- **BARBARA MARSH** TO THE BONEYARD
- **MARIELA GRIFFOR** THE PSYCHIATRIST
- **DON SHARE** UNION
- **SHEILA HILLIER** HOTEL MOONMILK
- **FLOYD SKLOOT** CLOSE READING
- **PENNY BOXALL** SHIP OF THE LINE
- **MANDY KAHN** MATH, HEAVEN, TIME
- **MARION MCCREADY** TREE LANGUAGE
- **RUFO QUINTAVALLE** WEATHER DERIVATIVES
- **SJ FOWLER** THE ROTTWEILER'S GUIDE TO THE DOG OWNER
- **TEDI LÓPEZ MILLS** DEATH ON RUA AUGUSTA
- **AGNIESZKA STUDZINSKA** WHAT THINGS ARE
- **JEMMA BORG** THE ILLUMINATED WORLD
- **KEIRAN GODDARD** FOR THE CHORUS
- **COLETTE SENSIER** SKINLESS

EYEWEAR PROSE

- **SUMIA SUKKAR** THE BOY FROM ALEPPO WHO PAINTED THE WAR
- **ALFRED CORN** MIRANDA'S BOOK

EYEWEAR LITERARY CRITICISM

- **MARK FORD** THIS DIALOGUE OF ONE